# HEA
# WHISPERS

## BENEDICTINE
## WISDOM
## FOR TODAY

---

# LEADER'S
# GUIDE

---

## ELIZABETH J. CANHAM

---

UPPER
ROOM BOOKS
Nashville

HEART WHISPERS
*Leader's Guide*
Copyright © 1999 by Elizabeth J. Canham
All rights reserved.

The Upper Room® Website http://www.upperroom.org

Scripture quotations not otherwise identified are from the New Revised Standard Version of the Bible, copyright © 1989 by the Division of Christian Education, National Council of the Churches of Christ in the United States of America. Used by permission.

All scripture quotations designated BCP are taken from the *Book of Common Prayer* (Episcopal), published by The Church Hymnal Corporation, New York, 1979.

All scripture quotations designated AP is the author's paraphrase.

Cover design: Gore Studio, Inc.
Cover transparency: © Mark Lewis / Picturesque
Second printing: 2000

Printed in the United States of America

# CONTENTS

# I

# INTRODUCTION

We live in a heart-hungry world. Bombarded by noise, slogans, and advertising we sometimes grow deaf to the life-giving good news the scriptures contain. Perhaps we hear the Bible read in church or we choose a personal devotional time each day but experience difficulty when we try to take in what the words mean to us in our time. This course is designed to enable us to slow down, to practice listening at a deeper level to God who always speaks graciously, generously, and intimately to each of us. Our focus will be on attentive listening as we allow the messages of scripture to move from head to heart. Saint Benedict's Rule will guide us along this way of heart listening.

Thank you for your desire to offer leadership to other pilgrims who also yearn to hear more clearly what the spirit is saying today. You do not need an advanced theological education in order to provide the kind of guidance anticipated in this book. Many of the first Benedictine monks were unable to read, but they had a deep desire to follow Christ as they looked for support and accountability within the community. You will need a similar hunger to grow in Christ, a willingness to listen to God and others, and a commitment to prayerful preparation for each of the weekly sessions.

Ideally the final session should be planned as a more extensive retreat time, preferably an overnight or weekend gathering. If this is impossible, then a day of reflection may be designed. You *will* need to give thought to this before beginning the course so that participants will know what is expected and what costs may be involved. Please read the notes for Session Ten at this time since you will need to make arrangements and continue planning throughout the course. Throughout the book you will find quotes from the Rule of Saint Benedict. You may wish to purchase a copy of the Rule for your own use, and I suggest the following: *The Rule of Saint Benedict in English*, edited by Timothy Fry, OSB (Liturgical Press, Collegeville, Minn., 1981). A second valuable source book is *The Rule of Benedict: Insights for the Ages* by Joan D. Chittister (New York: Crossroad, 1993). This book translates significant sections of the Rule into more inclusive language and offers reflections on various topics. In the Order for Compline, which begins on page 42, an asterisk (*) within a psalm indicates the place where congregants may respond with the portion of the verse that follows.

I have used the New Revised Standard Version of the Bible for all quotations from scripture except for the psalms, where I have opted for the translation from the Episcopal *Book of Common Prayer* (New York: Church Hymnal Corporations, 1979). Of course you are free to use any biblical text you choose, and participants may be invited to bring their chosen versions since variation can add richness to understanding of scripture.

The design of Session One assumes that members of the group have a copy of *Heart Whispers* and have read the Introduction and first chapter, "Praying the Scriptures." This means planning well in advance of the course beginning and obtaining copies of the book for distribution.

# II
# FORMING A GROUP

The ideal group size for this design is six to twelve participants. If you plan to offer the course to a larger number, plan for additional leadership for smaller breakout groups, especially for the community *lectio divina*. Be clear in your advertising of the course that a commitment to all sessions is important since the community that forms allows for a deep trust level to develop, which can be interrupted by people coming and going. Also make sure that each person a) has a copy of the book and b) understands that reading and preparation are an important part of the course. You might choose to formulate a covenant agreement that each participant signs (see sample below). This could be incorporated into worship on the evening of your first gathering, like the monks in Saint Benedict's monastery who signed an agreement to abide by the Rule and placed it on the altar in the presence of the gathered community.

## *A Heart Listening Covenant*

I, _____(name)_____, desire to listen to God "with the ear of my heart" in community with _____ group. I will, to the best of my ability, be present at each session and undertake to read assigned passages and complete exercises. I will pray for members of the group and will keep a daily journal to help me increase awareness of God's word spoken through scripture, nature, and daily experience.

_____        _____
Signed                                                              Date

Be aware of the space in which you will meet and make it as hospitable as possible. An ugly room can be transformed by some color and living things. I usually choose to create an "altar," a table covered with a colorful spread incorporating plants, a candle, and other objects of beauty. Participants can contribute by bringing items of importance to them in prayer and adding them to the centerpiece. You might want to have beverages or snacks available, though it is good to encourage a quiet entering of the meeting space rather than general chit-chat over coffee. If a meal or other social time precedes the meeting, maybe it could take place in a different room. Quiet music playing as people enter the space can help set the tone for the session.

# III

# SESSION STRUCTURE

Each session will contain the following:

- Preparation
- Gathering for Prayer and Sharing
- Meditation/Reflection Exercise
- Passage for Group *Lectio Divina*
- Closing Worship

Allow at least two hours for each session. After the first week invite participants to share their experience of heart listening since the last meeting. This may include insights that emerge from the *lectio divina* assigned for the current chapter, awareness of God's "speaking" through life experience, nature, and so forth. Be sure participants understand that no one is *required* to speak, and request that any shared personal experience remain within the group. You may need to limit each person's sharing, especially if some participants tend to be loquacious!

Each group will vary in the allotment of time to each section of the session, but you will need at least thirty minutes for the opening time. The meditation/reflection exercise will usually take about thirty minutes and group *lectio divina* about forty-five minutes. Allow about fifteen minutes for closing worship.

Discourage too much discussion at this time by reminding the group that the primary task is to *listen.* A brief affirming word can be more important than becoming sidetracked into personal reminiscences generated by another's speaking. Also remember that when participants speak of problems with prayer, disappointments, or difficult family tensions, you are not there to "fix" the difficulties. You may choose to "flag" some issues to address in future sessions. If someone talks of distractions during prayer time or difficulty with the discipline of daily journal writing, make a mental note to deal with these specific issues later. You may offer individual help at another time or refer the person to a professional if you sense that he or she is dealing with issues that require pastoral or psychological counseling.

Each weekly session will include the following form of group *lectio divina*, which derives from a type of Bible study called the African Model. This model developed on that continent to enable small groups to listen and relate scripture to specific life situations. Emphasize at the beginning that *lectio divina* does not entail a general discussion of the passage but rather a listening to hear what speaks to each person *now* in his or her life journey. Encourage the use of "I" statements, which avoid generalization or preaching. Reassure the group members that the closing prayer time need not make them uncomfortable. Explain that the hand-holding simply allows persons to feel safe since it takes away the requirement that they speak prayers aloud. In my experience even those who have never prayed publicly choose to do so in this context, especially when they feel no coercion.

*

# GROUP
# LECTIO DIVINA

1) Begin with a few moments of silent prayer.

2) Ask one person to read the scripture aloud, slowly.

3) Ask participants to name silently a word or phrase to themselves that caught their attention (1 minute).

4) Invite each member to share the word or phrase with the group. (Be brief—do not elaborate, explain, or teach; members offer sharing to the group, not the leader.)

5) Ask a group member to read aloud the scripture again.

6) Ask each person to take three to five minutes silently naming or writing down where this passage touches his or her life today.

7) Invite each to share the above, beginning with an I-statement.

8) Ask another participant to read the scripture aloud once more.

9) Ask each again to silently name or write down responses to the following: From what I have heard and shared, what does God want me to do or be this week? How does God invite me to change?

10) Invite each to share the above beginning with "I...."

11) To close, all stand. Each participant prays for the person on his or her right, either silently or aloud, naming what that person shared in step 10. Participants hold hands so that those who choose to pray in silence may squeeze the hand of the person on the right to indicate that prayer has been offered.

# PRAYING THE SCRIPTURES

## *Preparation*

- Prepare a name tag for each person.
- Bring an audiotape or CD player and play quiet music as people enter the meeting room.
- Place a Bible and candle on the central "altar."
- Place chairs in a circle.
- Ask persons prior to the session to bring an object (photo, toy, pine cone, rock, jewelry) that has been significant to them on their faith journey.

## *Gathering for Prayer and Sharing*

Welcome the group and deal with any practical issues (location of restrooms, availability of refreshments). Begin the sharing process by modeling the method: Tell the participants who you are and why you are leading the group. Offer a brief statement about your faith journey illustrated by the object you have brought. Place the object on the altar and invite the group to take turns sharing around the circle. When each person has spoken, offer a brief prayer of thanksgiving for the gathering and commitment to being together.

- Take a brief stretch break.

## Meditation/Reflection Exercise

It is important to recognize that we pray with our bodies as
well as our minds. Listening prayer becomes more possible
when we feel *alert* and *relaxed*. The following exercise enables
a letting go of tension, anxiety, or busy thoughts and prepares
our bodies for prayer. First invite participants to sit comfort-
ably, feet on floor, hands loosely resting on their laps, and to
take several deep breaths. Then offer the following, speaking
slowly and allowing time between each statement:

> Now I invite you to close your eyes....Continue to
> breathe deeply....As you exhale, let go of tension,
> anxiety, unfinished business....As you inhale, receive
> the spirit or breath of God into your deepest be-
> ing....Keep breathing....Be aware of how your body
> feels....We are going to pay attention to our bodies,
> relaxing each part in turn....Begin with your feet; are
> they comfortable, at rest? Let go of any tension....Now
> relax your calves...relax your thighs....Be aware of
> both legs relaxed....Keep breathing....Be aware of the
> chair that supports you....Relax your hips...
> abdomen...chest....Relax your shoulders, where you
> carry so much tension....Let your hands relax and your
> arms....Pay attention to your breathing....Relax the
> muscles of your throat and neck...relax your jaw
> ...relax your face and scalp....Take a moment to be
> aware again of your body. Do you notice any changes?
> ...If you feel tension somewhere, relax again and let it
> go....As you continue to breathe deeply notice the
> sounds that reach you... sounds outside...sounds in
> the room...the sound of your own breath....Now
> allow those sounds just to be there without demand-
> ing attention....Don't try to block them out, just let
> them be....Now listen as I read some words of scrip
> ture to you several times....Continue to listen in the

pauses between reading, letting the word speak to you as God chooses…. "Those who wait for the Lord shall renew their strength, they shall mount up with wings like eagles, they shall run and not be weary, they shall walk and not faint."

[*Repeat text.*]

[*Repeat text.*]

…Be aware of how you feel as you hear this scripture; are you hopeful, encouraged, anxious, peaceful?…As you listen one more time, allow yourself to respond silently to God by expressing need, gratitude, intercession, confession, adoration….

[*Repeat text.*]

…Now as we come to the end of this meditation, be aware of the chair supporting you….Notice sounds ….Allow yourself to remember others in the room with you….When you are ready, open your eyes and take in once again this time and place as you savor the moments of listening.

At the end of the meditation, invite comments on the experience; how did relaxation of the body enhance the participants' listening? What did they hear?

At this point brief discussion is appropriate, and some of the attitudes toward scripture explored in chapter 1 may be raised. At the conclusion encourage participants to adapt this relaxation exercise for use before their personal prayer time and to notice any changes that occur as a result of paying attention to the body.

### Passage for Group Lectio Divina
### John 2:1-11

At the close of the group *lectio divina* remind everyone to read the chapter on Hospitality before the next gathering.

## Closing Worship

1) Gather the community with music. You may choose an audiotape or CD or invite someone to provide music. Singing a hymn or chant together is also appropriate.

2) Offer prayer for the group.

3) Invite each person to sign his or her covenant and place it on the altar, saying, "I ask for the prayers of this community that I may listen to God with the ear of my heart." (*Print this sentence legibly on a sheet of paper and put it on the altar before worship.*) Again model this exercise by placing your covenant on the altar first.

4) When all have come forward, stand in a circle and conclude with a statement about the group's commitment. For example, "Saint Benedict invited those who yearned for God to listen with their hearts to scripture and to place themselves under a Rule of life that included prayer, study, work, recreation, and community time. We have come together as God's people to make our commitment to God and to one another so that we too may grow in faith, hope, and love. May God bless, strengthen, and keep us in these weeks together and give us much joy through faithful listening. Go in peace to love and serve God. Amen."

# HOSPITALITY

## *Preparation*

- Bring an audiotape or CD player and quiet music.
- Prepare the altar and include on it a loaf of bread and some grapes.
- Arrange the room as before.

## *Gathering for Prayer and Sharing*

Allow the group to gather quietly as they listen to music. Offer a prayer of thanksgiving and expectation. Then take one to two minutes to speak of your own experience of heart listening since the group first met. Don't be afraid to mention any difficulties you may have had, since this will encourage others to speak of any resistance or blocks to prayer that they have had. Invite each member of the group to share his or her experience.

## *Meditation/Reflection Exercise*

While everyone is seated in the circle, invite each person to be aware that she or he is a beloved child of God and to hear that assurance in scripture: "Blessed be the God and Father of our Lord Jesus Christ, who has blessed us in Christ with every spiritual blessing in the heavenly places, just as he chose us in Christ before the foundation of the world to be holy and blameless before him in love. He destined us for adoption as his children through Jesus Christ" (Eph. 1:3-5).

Now ask the group members to look at one another, to

recognize the belovedness, chosenness, and giftedness of each one. Ask them not to fear eye contact, even if it feels unnatural in the beginning. Invite them to identify one quality or gift they see in each person. Then ask them to stand and move around the room. As individuals meet, invite them to speak their appreciation of the other's presence in the following way: "( *Name* ), I appreciate your ( *name gift or quality* ) and know you are beloved by God." Examples of gifts might include a smile, gentleness, integrity, listening, compassion, etc. When all have met and spoken to one another, ask that they return to their seats and to say how it felt to be greeted in this way. Ask them to consider how their congregations might enhance hospitality by affirming others' gifts through verbal appreciation. Mention that even those persons to whom we may not be drawn have some quality or gift to celebrate.

## Passage for Group Lectio Divina
### John 6:35-40

Remind the group to read the chapter on Simplicity before the next meeting.

## Closing Worship

Jesus was frequently present at meals, accepting the hospitality of many different people. His final words to the disciples were spoken at a meal we have come to call the Last Supper, and the early Christian church broke bread together as its members became a community and celebrated what Christ had come to mean to them. The Agape, or love feast, provided an opportunity for Christians to receive food with gratitude and to remember what Christ had done for them in making them beloved children of God. The closing worship for this session on Hospitality may take the form of an Agape during which the bread and grapes from the altar are shared and commitment to hospitable living is reaffirmed.

Adapt the following form to the group's needs:

1)  Offer a gathering prayer.

2)  Lead the group in a song, hymn, or chant.

3)  Explain to the group that the early Christian community met to share a "love feast" (Agape) in memory of Jesus. In time this kind of gathering took on a more liturgical form as Holy Communion. Jesus became known to grieving disciples in the breaking of bread (Luke 24:35).

4)  Take the bread from the altar and pass it around the group, inviting each person to break off a piece to eat. You might offer a statement such as, "Bread for the journey," as the bread is passed.

5)  Share the grapes in a similar way and again you may offer a statement such as, "The fruit of the earth to sustain you."

6)  When all have eaten, offer a concluding prayer. Consider using the following: "Gracious God, you have called all of us to be your beloved children; you always welcome us no matter how we come to you. Thank you for sustaining us with the gifts of the earth and the generosity of your people. Above all we bless you for all you give to us through Christ the Bread of Life. Now send us out to be your people in the world that others may be drawn into the circle. Amen."

# SIMPLICITY

## *Preparation*

- Bring an audiotape or CD player and quiet music.
- Gather leaves of various kinds and place them in a bowl or basket on the altar.
- Arrange the room as before.

## *Gathering for Prayer and Sharing*

Before beginning remind participants that in the final part of group *lectio divina,* persons name a specific need or action and the prayer that follows attempts to support them in following through with that identified need. What responses have they experienced to those prayers? Encourage them to share aloud if they feel comfortable doing so.

## *Meditation/Reflection Exercise*

Tell the group members that you will lead them in a meditation that uses the senses to deepen awareness and prayer. If people have mentioned distractions or difficulty with maintaining focus, you might tell them that this exercise may particularly help them with such problems and that they may practice it at home. Explain that the exercise will have three parts with silence between each part. If they choose, participants may write their response at the end of the exercise.

1) Pass the basket or bowl of leaves around the circle and ask each person to take one.

2) Invite the group members to focus on the leaves, paying attention to shape, texture, color, smell, and even sound as they hold and move it. Tell them simply to observe, to pay

attention to the leaf, and to keep coming back to it if the mind begins to wander. Allow about two minutes for this phase.

3) Now suggest that as they continue to hold and observe the leaf, they allow their minds freely to associate ideas, memories, images, biblical stories suggested by the leaf. This time encourage participants to go wherever their thoughts take them and not to be afraid of too many associations. Allow three to four minutes for this.

4) This time ask group members to identify the strongest image, memory, idea, or biblical story or the one around which they feel the most energy and to stay with that one image, memory, or idea. Ask what it teaches them about God, about their experience, about prayer. At this point those who wish to do so may write their response. Allow four to five minutes.

5) Finally, invite silent prayer as each person takes the message of the leaf and translates it into a response to God, be that thanksgiving, intercession, adoration, repentance.

6) Invite the participants to share their insights with the group, and again model this sharing yourself.

### Passage for Group Lectio Divina
Luke 18:18-25

Remind the group to read the chapter on Prayer before the next meeting.

### Closing Worship

Often our worship is "busy"and full of words because we fear silence. The simple closing worship will focus primarily on silence and an invitation to the participants to notice their feelings about the absence of structure. If you have access to the old Shaker song "'Tis a Gift to Be Simple," you might begin by singing or playing it. Since many people have difficulty with silence, limit the time; five minutes is probably enough to begin with. At the close of this time of silence, you might invite prayers or brief statements about insights gained. Close with a brief prayer, or use the following: "Loving Creator, help us simplify our lives and trust more in your grace. Amen."

# PRAYER

## *Preparation*

- Bring an audiotape or CD player and quiet music.
- Place incense or a scented candle on the altar.
- Arrange the room as before.

## *Gathering for Prayer and Sharing*

Follow the suggestions for the previous session.

## *Meditation/Reflection Exercise*

Today we consider an ancient prayer form based on the repetition of a word or phrase—a "mantra" prayer. The "Jesus Prayer," dating back to at least the sixth century C.E., is the oldest known Christian mantra, used consistently since that time.

The Jesus Prayer takes two forms:

Lord Jesus Christ,
Son of the living God,
Have mercy on me,
a sinner.

or

Lord Jesus Christ,
Have mercy on me.

Persons repeated the prayer over and over with the desire that prayer move from head to heart. This rhythmic prayer is not vain repetition but, like the waves of the ocean, can move the one praying to a quiet, calm, listening place. I find the shorter Jesus prayer the perfect accompaniment to walking or swimming, and I use it often in waiting situations or while driving. To introduce the idea of mantra prayer to the group, you might use the Jesus Prayer or a biblical phrase, such as, "For God alone my soul in silence waits"; "The Lord is my shepherd"; "Come, Lord Jesus." Another possibility would involve the use of a recorded chant that the group could sing repetitively. The chants used by the Taizé Community are ideal for group chanting. Begin the mantra or chant together for several minutes and then allow for silence. You may wish to ring a bell to indicate the end of the silence. Be sensitive to the experience of the group and begin with a *short* silence of about five minutes. Invite the group to discuss the experience, and encourage the members to try mantra prayer during the coming week.

### Passage for Group Lectio Divina
### Mark 1:35-39

Remind the group to read the chapter on Manual Labor before the next meeting.

### Closing Worship

The last Office of the day in monastic communities is Compline in which the community lets go of the day's activities and commits the sleeping hours to God. It would be appropriate to use this night Office (see Appendix) or to substitute another form of night prayer from a different denominational worship book. Begin by lighting the scented candle or incense and saying these words: "Let my prayer be set forth in your sight as incense, / the lifting up of my hands as the evening sacrifice" (Ps. 141:2, BCP). Then move on to follow the order of Compline as indicated in the Appendix.

# MANUAL LABOR

## *Preparation*

- Bring an audiotape or CD player and quiet music.
- Prepare a ball of clay (or play dough) for each person, along with paper towels and several damp cloths.
- Arrange the room as before.

## *Gathering for Prayer and Sharing*

Follow the procedure established in previous weeks.

## *Meditation/Reflection Exercise*

Distribute the clay balls to the participants. Tell them that today's meditation will put them in touch with their creativity, but that *they do not need to be artists* to participate. They begin with a ball of clay, and they may choose to end with a ball of clay. The point is, like Benedict's monks, to work with their hands, allowing this activity to become prayer. Suggest that participants select a place to be with their clay—elsewhere in the room or outside—but to avoid conversation. Set a time limit of fifteen to twenty minutes for the experience. Tell them that they will have an opportunity to discuss the experience and to place their creation on the altar if they so choose. Decide whether you wish to have music playing. Read selections from Genesis 1 and suggest that participants be aware that they are made in God's image; they too are creators. Provide paper towels and damp cloths for cleaning up. At the end of the assigned time, regroup and share comments and creations.

## Group Lectio Divina
### Matthew 4:18-22

Remind the group to read the chapter on Rest before the next meeting.

## Closing Worship

At this point in the study, you might feel comfortable asking others to take responsibility for closing worship. Suggest that for the next meeting one person write some prayers, one or more choose readings (not necessarily biblical) that focus on rest, and encourage another to create a simple ritual for use in worship. Ask participants to bring a blanket and pillow next week.

You might use the following verses as an invitation to worship:

Show your servants your works
    and your splendor to their children.
May the graciousness of the Lord our God be upon us;
    prosper the work of our hands;
    prosper our handiwork.
                        —Psalm: 90:16-17, BCP

Then say this prayer aloud: "Holy One, we see you hard at work in the world about us bringing forth newness and revealing beauty in all that you have made. We are grateful that you work in our lives also, and we recognize that you call us to become agents of change where injustice, oppression, and fear dominate. Give us ready hands, compassionate hearts, and courageous willingness to work for the coming of your reign of peace. Amen."

Invite the group to name places and experiences in which they have seen God at work today, such as in the smile of another, the healing of a relationship, answered prayer, beauty of nature, news report of hope. End with one of the Compline prayers that reminds us that others work while we rest.

# SESSION SIX

# REST

## *Preparation*

- Bring an audiotape or CD player and quiet music.
- Have several extra pillows and blankets available.
- Arrange the room as before.

## *Gathering for Prayer and Sharing*

Proceed as in previous weeks.

## *Meditation/Reflection Exercise*

Sometimes even our prayer times are busy, hard work. Tell the members that they will not have to use their minds in this exercise but simply rest in God, letting go of tension and anxiety. Invite each person to find a space in the room to spread out a blanket and then to assume a comfortable resting posture. Encourage those unable to lie down on the floor to get as comfortable as they can while sitting and relaxing.

Remind participants of the first relaxation exercise in which they relaxed each part of the body. Suggest that they again pay attention to their bodies, noticing their breathing and consciously releasing tension. You might suggest that they allow themselves to go back in time, to imagine themselves in kindergarten with no responsibilities at nap time! Assure the group that if someone falls asleep it will not be regarded as failure but as God's gift.

To begin the resting meditation you might use the aria

from Mendelssohn's *Elijah* , "Oh rest in the Lord," or read Psalm 116:6. Draw the meditation gently to a close, allowing time to move from resting to regathering in the circle. Allow a few minutes of discussion; ask if participants see ways they might incorporate this kind of restful being in God's presence into their personal prayer time.

## Passage for Group Lectio Divina
### Luke 10:38-42

Remind the group to read the chapter on Stability before the next meeting.

## Closing Worship

Before the worship time begins, ask the members to consider writing psalms on the theme of stability for use in next week's closing. They could take the structure of an existing psalm and develop new words, thereby creating contemporary psalmody. Some psalms that particularly lend themselves to this approach are 11; 16; 18; 27; 46. You may also assign someone to lead prayers or offer musical accompaniment.

Move into the closing worship as led by the group.

# SESSION SEVEN

## STABILITY

### *Preparation*

- Bring an audiotape or CD player and quiet music.
- Make available paper, crayons or markers.
- Arrange the room as before.

### *Gathering for Prayer and Sharing*

Proceed as in previous weeks.

### *Meditation/Reflection Exercise*

Give each group member a sheet of paper and make crayons or markers available. Again reassure participants that this exercise requires no artistic skills and that you will not give grades! Ask the members to divide the paper into four sections and then to find a comfortable place to work while they complete the exercise. Quiet music can move this process along. Ask them to fill in the squares using the following statements (people can be stick figures):

1) "Draw a person who represented stability and security for you during childhood."

2) "Draw a place—perhaps a private, safe place—where you felt secure."

3) "Draw a symbol that represents stability for you today."

4) "Write a mantra statement on stability, for example, 'God is the ground of my being. I am anchored in God.'"

Set a clear time limit to complete the project—about fifteen to twenty minutes—and then regather. Invite participants to share their people, places, and symbols. To provide closure, go around the circle and invite each person to offer his or her mantra as prayer.

## Passage for Group Lectio Divina
### John 15:1-5

Remind the group to read the chapter on Conversion of Life before the next meeting.

## Closing Worship

Worship is led by the group. Ask for a volunteer to coordinate next week's concluding worship. He or she may choose to lead the group or involve others in worship focused on the theme of Conversion of Life. You will need to discuss this earlier with the group.

In preparation for the retreat (session 10), tell the group that the retreat model will make available longer periods for silence, prayer, and reflection. Encourage them to prepare for these changes by practicing silent time at home each day.

# CONVERSION OF LIFE

## *Preparation*

- Bring an audiotape or CD player and quiet music.
- Place a glass bowl of water and some short leafy branches (spruce or pine are ideal) on the altar.
- Have available a large candle or lantern.
- Arrange the room as before.

## *Gathering for Prayer and Sharing*

At the end of the time of sharing, ask participants if specific aspects of the course have been especially helpful; invite suggestions for addressing particular needs or issues. At this time remind them about the concluding retreat and ask them to begin their preparation for this event. You may have practical suggestions to offer, and their comments may impact the retreat design.

## *Meditation/Reflection Exercise*

A darkened room greatly increases the efficacy of this meditation. Place the large candle or lantern in the center of the room on a table or the altar, making sure that its light can be easily diffused.

Begin by reminding the participants that we are God's beloved, chosen to be the body of Christ in the world and united to Christ through our baptism. Next refer to the previous week's reading on conversion and point out that though we often fall short of our commitment to follow Christ, God is always waiting to welcome us home when we turn back. Read Luke 22:54-62.

Invite the group members to turn their chairs to face out of the circle. Light the candle or lantern, and turn off the lights. Now ask that they become aware of their shadows, of feelings of alienation generated by turning the back on others or God, and ask for silent prayers of repentance as they identify times when they have denied Christ through fear, busyness, or unwillingness to follow. Allow four to five minutes for this exercise. At the end of the reflection time, offer the following prayer of reassurance:

> Bless the Lord, O my soul,
>> and all that is within me, bless God's holy name.
> God forgives all our sins
>> and heals our weaknesses.
> —Psalm 103:1, 3, AP

Say to the group: "Let us with joy celebrate God's gracious, forgiving love and commit ourselves anew to the promises of baptism." Have the participants turn their chairs around to face one another in the circle. At this point you might choose to sing a chant, song, or hymn of praise. An appropriate hymn is, "Praise My Soul, the King of Heaven" with its assurance that we are "ransomed, healed, restored, forgiven." Now invite the group into a renewal of the baptismal promises using the following form or one provided in your denominational worship book.

LEADER    There is one Body and one Spirit;

PEOPLE    **There is one hope in God's call to us;**

LEADER    One Lord, one Faith, one Baptism;

PEOPLE    **One God and Father of all.**

LEADER    The Lord be with you.

PEOPLE    **And also with you.**

LEADER    Let us pray.

ALL       **Grant, O Lord, that all who are baptized into the death of Jesus Christ your Son may live in the power of his resurrection and look for him to come again in glory; who lives and reigns now and for ever. Amen.**

LEADER    Let us now renew the promises made at our baptism.

Do you renounce Satan and all the spiritual forces of wickedness that rebel against God?

PEOPLE    **I renounce them.**

LEADER    Do you renounce the evil powers of this world which corrupt and destroy the creatures of God?

PEOPLE    **I renounce them.**

LEADER    Do you renounce all sinful desires that draw you from the love of God?

PEOPLE    **I renounce them.**

LEADER    Do you renew your commitment to Jesus Christ?

PEOPLE    **I do, and with God's grace I will follow him as my Savior and Lord.**

LEADER    As we prepare to walk in the way of Christ with fresh hope and faith, let this water become for us the outward sign of this renewal. (*Lift the bowl of water and ask a member of the group to hold it as you offer these prayers.*)

We thank you, Almighty God, for the gift of water. Over it the Holy Spirit moved in the beginning of creation. Through it you led the children of Israel out of their bondage in Egypt into the land of promise. In it your Son Jesus received the baptism of John and was anointed by the Holy Spirit as the Messiah, the Christ, to lead us, through his death and resurrection, from the bondage of sin into everlasting life.

We thank you, Father, for the water of Baptism. In it we are buried with Christ in his death. By it we share in his resurrection. Through it we are reborn by the Holy Spirit. Therefore in joyful obedience to your Son, we were baptized and now renew our commitment to walk with him in newness of life. (*Take the branches and, dipping them in the water, shower the group with drops of water.*)

Go in the name of Christ to proclaim good news to all. Amen.*

Take a short stretch break at this point.

### Passage for Group Lectio Divina
2 Corinthians 5:17-20

Remind the group to read the chapter on Obedience before the next meeting. Provide a sheet for roommate sign-ups if the retreat occurs overnight.

### Closing Worship

Worship is led by the group. Next week's worship would most appropriately be a Communion service that emphasizes obedience to Jesus' words, "Do this in remembrance of me." If you do not have an ordained person in the group, you might ask a clergy person to be present to preside at this service.

---

*Adapted from *The Book of Common Prayer,* 1979 (Episcopal).

# SESSION NINE

# OBEDIENCE

## *Preparation*

- Bring an audiotape or CD player and quiet music.
- Collect and bring props for skits, such as drapes, hats, instruments (items found in childhood "dressup" boxes).
- Prepare a retreat information sheet for distribution.
- Arrange the room as before.

## *Gathering for Prayer and Sharing*

Proceed as in previous weeks.

## *Meditation/Reflection Exercise*

Form small groups of no more than six persons. Ask each group to prepare a short skit that illustrates ways we might be called upon to obey God in contemporary life situations. You might suggest the following ideas to spur their thoughts: getting up early enough for prayer, refusing to lie at work, speaking up for the Christian faith. Encourage them to use their imaginations and props as needed, to allow for laughter as well as serious moments. Allow twenty minutes to prepare the skits; then invite each group to present its offering. After the skits, discuss the real-life issues presented and help participants articulate ways in which they choose to become more aware of obedience to God in everyday life.

## *Passage for Group Lectio Divina*
### Philippians 2:5-11

Remind the group to read the chapter on Pilgrimage prior to next week's retreat. Before the closing worship, distribute the retreat information sheets. Briefly highlight details, such as arrangements, times, place, and necessary items. Make sure that members of the group have the telephone number of the retreat location for use in case of emergency. Confirm roommate assignments. Tell the group members that their pilgrimage to the retreat meeting place begins when they leave home; ask them to be conscious of their feelings as they make their way to the facility.

## *Closing Worship*
Close with a Communion service.

# LIFE AS PILGRIMAGE

## *Preparation*

Much of the preparation for this final session will depend on the place and timing for the retreat. The following guidelines will assist your planning.

- Decide on the length of retreat. If you make overnight plans, find a suitable center to accommodate the group.

- Try to find a quiet location away from your usual meeting place if you only have one day. Maybe members of your congregation have a country home to offer. Choose an ample space with places for short walks.

- Decide on your gathering place and if possible visit it ahead of time so you can decide how to enhance the space. You may want to ask others to bring pictures, fresh flowers or plants, an icon or painting, large cushions. If you plan to use hymns and/or liturgical resources, make sure you bring adequate books and a musician.

- Consider the need for childcare arrangements and plan accordingly.

- Decide how to handle meals and snacks if the facility does not provide them. Consider having someone cater the event, or ask group members to bring assigned dishes and snacks. Keep the menu simple to cut down on preparation time during the retreat.

- Line up transportation. If any group members have handicapping conditions, be sure they can access the facility.

- Greet each person in a hospitable manner upon arrival. (Benedict chose a wise old monk as porter. Who might be the best welcomer among you?) You may choose to have a small bag or basket of goodies for each person that contains items and food, such as candy, bubble bath, a pen, natural objects for reflection, Bible verses.

- Ask participants to bring the collages they made following their reading of the Pilgrimage chapter.

- Discourage members from receiving telephone calls during the retreat time.

- Bring necessary supplies: newsprint board, paper, paints, crayons, markers, scissors, glue, clay.

Adapt the following suggested schedules to meet the unique needs of your group.

### Schedule A: One-Day Retreat

9:30 AM    Gathering time and welcome. Have coffee and other beverages, fresh fruit and muffins available.

9:45       Worship

10:00      First session

10:30      Personal quiet time, journaling, and *lectio divina*

11:30      Second session

12:15 PM   Prayers

12:30      Lunch (silent meal with music in background)

1:15       Group *lectio divina*

2:00       Exploring creativity

4:00       Worship and sharing of creativity
           Closure

## *Schedule B: Weekend Retreat*

**Friday**

| | |
|---|---|
| 6:30 PM | Gathering time and welcome |
| 7:00 | Supper |
| 8:00 | First session |
| 9:00 | Compline |

**Saturday**

| | |
|---|---|
| 8:00 AM | Breakfast |
| 8:45 | Silent meditation |
| 9:00 | Second session |
| 9:45 | Personal quiet time, journaling, and *lectio divina* |
| 12:15 PM | Prayers |
| 12:30 | Lunch (silent meal with music in background) |
| 1:15 | Group *lectio divina* |
| 2:00 | Exploring creativity |
| 4:00 | Worship and sharing of creativity |

Closure or if continuing through Sunday, allow longer for afternoon activity and offer evening worship and sharing at 5:00 PM followed by supper. Evening activity might include singing, video on some aspect of prayer and discipleship, visiting speaker/artist or more quiet time. On Sunday morning worship may follow breakfast (Holy Communion if possible) and Closure.

## *Gathering and Welcome*

Deal with practical matters and concerns before beginning worship. Remind the group members that this time is a gift, lovingly offered by God who speaks to our hearts when we come apart to listen. Congratulate the group for prioritizing this time and taking care of so many details in order to get away from schedules and responsibilities. Invite them to expect God's blessing of the time and ask that they avoid setting agendas. The time of retreat requires only a gentle openness to the Creator.

## Worship

Begin the retreat with a hymn or chant, prayer, and scripture reading. (Genesis 12:1-9 is suggested.)

## First Session

Invite the group members to share the collages they made illustrating their life pilgrimages after you have offered yours. Others may add words of encouragement and appreciation to each person but avoid lengthy discussion. At the end of the sharing, ask participants to name the blessings and lessons learned through this exercise and record these on newsprint. Some possible comments might include, "God was with me in dark times"; "I experienced grace unexpectedly"; "Others reached out to me."

Now invite participants to remember what they have named as they go into silence.

## Personal Quiet Time, Journaling, and Lectio Divina

Suggest that each person find a quiet and inviting place and enter the silence, taking with him or her a Bible, journal, and pen. Suggest that participants reflect on the following questions (you may put them on newsprint or have them on a handout).

- Where am I at this moment on my pilgrimage?
- What do I need to leave behind so that I can travel light?
- What gift do I need from God to enable me to continue faithfully?

The only rule for this time is that participants honor the

silence. They may choose a scripture passage to help their reflection; spend some time walking or meditating outside; write prayers, psalms, poetry. Remind them that if the silence brings discomfort, they may choose to explore their feelings by writing about them.

## Second Session

This session offers an opportunity not only to share experience but to enhance listening skills. Tell the group that the following exercise enables them to support and help one another listen more attentively to God and others. Form trios and tell participants that each person will have an opportunity to be a listener, speaker, and observer. Explain the following roles:

1) Speaker—For five minutes the speaker addresses the listener, relating his or her experience of participating in this course: blessings received, lessons learned, friendships established.

2) Listener—The listener does not interrupt or speak but simply listens attentively to what is said. A smile or nod of encouragement is appropriate. At the end of five minutes, the listener tells the speaker what he or she heard, that is, reflects what was shared.

3) Observer—The observer keeps track of time and observes the interaction between speaker and listener, noticing emotional response, attention or inattention, warmth, "body language," empathy. When the listener has finished reflecting back what he or she heard, the observer shares observations of both of them.

Emphasize that we undertake this exercise to encourage each of us to be better listeners. Each person will have the opportunity to participate in the three roles. At the end of the exercise, gather the whole group and ask for learnings, again noting them on newsprint.

## Exploring Creativity

During the course the group has experienced a number of different activities using the medium of art. At this time participants give free rein to imagination and allow it to guide them. If weather and environment permit, you might suggest that they first spend some time out-of-doors, allowing nature to inspire imagination and perhaps taking time to collect natural objects for use in the art project. Someone may choose to dance, another to observe ants, someone else to climb a tree. Encourage the freedom to move, sit, or begin working immediately with clay or paint. Perhaps a multimedia project will emerge; a poem or hymn be written. Allow this to be playful time. Decide whether or not to suggest silence. If total silence seems inappropriate, suggest that "small talk" might deflect from allowing creativity to be a means through which we listen.

## Passage for Group Lectio Divina
### Hebrews 12:1-6

## Closure

Think carefully about closure. You may want to invite each person to write a personal commitment to continue her or his faith journey and to place that on the altar in the same way the group members offered their covenants at the beginning of the course. An ongoing group may emerge but be clear that no one is expected to join. Be creative; consider inviting others to join you in designing a closing ritual.

# APPENDIX

# AN ORDER FOR COMPLINE

THE OFFICIANT BEGINS
The Lord Almighty grant us a peaceful night and a perfect end. Amen.

Our help is in the Name of the Lord;

PEOPLE
The maker of heaven and earth.

THE OFFICIANT MAY THEN SAY
Let us confess our sins to God.

*Silence may be kept.*

OFFICIANT AND PEOPLE
Almighty God, our heavenly Father:
We have sinned against you,
through our own fault,
in thought, and word, and deed,
and in what we have left undone.
For the sake of your Son our Lord Jesus Christ,
forgive us all our offenses;
and grant that we may serve you
in newness of life,
to the glory of your Name. Amen.

OFFICIANT
May the Almighty God grant us forgiveness of all our sins, and the grace and comfort of the Holy Spirit. *Amen.*

THE OFFICIANT THEN SAYS

O God, make speed to save us.

PEOPLE

O Lord, make haste to help us.

OFFICIANT AND PEOPLE

Glory to the Father, and to the Son, and to the Holy Spirit: as it was in the beginning, is now, and will be for ever. Amen.

*Except in Lent, add* Alleluia.

*One or more of the following Psalms are sung or said. Other suitable selections may be substituted.*

## Psalm 4    *Cum invocarem*

1   Answer me when I call, O God, defender of my cause;*
      you set me free when I am hard-pressed;
      have mercy on me and hear my prayer.

2   "You mortals, how long will you dishonor my glory?*
      how long will you worship dumb idols
      and run after false gods?"

3   Know that the LORD does wonders for the faithful;*
      when I call upon the LORD, he will hear me.

4   Tremble, then, and do not sin;*
      speak to your heart in silence upon your bed.

5   Offer the appointed sacrifices*
      and put your trust in the LORD.

6   Many are saying,
      "Oh, that we might see better times!"*
      Lift up the light of your countenance upon us, O LORD.

7   You have put gladness in my heart,*
      more than when grain and wine and oil increase.

HEART
WHISPERS

LEADER'S
GUIDE

8 I lie down in peace; at once I fall asleep;*
>for only you, Lord, make me dwell in safety.

**Psalm 31**   *In te, Domine, speravi*

1   In you, O Lord, have I taken refuge;
let me never be put to shame:*
>deliver me in your righteousness.

2   Incline your ear to me:*
>make haste to deliver me.

3   Be my strong rock, a castle to keep me safe,
for you are my crag and my stronghold;*
>for the sake of your Name, lead me and guide me.

4   Take me out of the net that they have secretly set for
me,*
>for you are my tower of strength.

5   Into your hands I commend my spirit,*
>for you have redeemed me,
>O Lord, O God of truth.

**Psalm 134**   *Ecce nunc*

1   Behold now, bless the Lord, all you servants of the
Lord,*
>you that stand by night in the house of the Lord.

2   Lift up your hands in the holy place and bless the
Lord;*
>the Lord who made heaven and earth bless you
out of Zion.

*At the end of the psalms sing or say*

Glory to the Father, and to the Son, and to the Holy
Spirit:*
>as it was in the beginning, is now, and will be
for ever. *Amen.*

*One of the following, or some other suitable passage of Scripture, is read:*

> Lord, you are in the midst of us, and we are called by
> your Name: Do not forsake us, O Lord our God
> *Jeremiah 14:9, 22.*

PEOPLE
Thanks be to God.

*or this:*

> Come to me, all who labor and are heavy-laden, and I
> will give you rest. Take my yoke upon you, and learn
> from me; for I am gentle and lowly in heart, and you
> will find rest for your souls. For my yoke is easy, and
> my burden is light. *Matthew 11:28-30*

PEOPLE
Thanks be to God.

*Or the following:*

> May the God of peace, who brought again from the
> dead our Lord Jesus, the great shepherd of the sheep, by
> the blood of the eternal covenant, equip you with
> everything good that you may do his will, working in
> you that which is pleasing in his sight, through Jesus
> Christ; to whom be glory for ever and ever. *Hebrews
> 13:20-21*

PEOPLE
Thanks be to God.

*Or this:*

> Be sober, be watchful. Your adversary the devil prowls
> around life a roaring lion, seeking someone to devour.
> Resist him, firm in your faith. *1 Peter 5.8-9a*

PEOPLE
Thanks be to God.

*A hymn suitable for the evening may be sung. Then follows:*

Versicle:  Into your hands, O Lord, I commend my spirit;

Response:  For you have redeemed me, O Lord, O God of
truth.

Versicle:  Keep us, O Lord, as the apple of your eye;

Response:  Hide us under the shadow of your wings.

Lord, have mercy.
*Christ, have mercy.*
Lord have mercy.

OFFICIANT AND PEOPLE
[Recite The Lord's Prayer together aloud.]

OFFICIANT
Lord, hear our prayer;

PEOPLE
And let our cry come to you.

OFFICIANT
Let us pray.

*The Officiant then says one of the following collects:*

Be our light in the darkness, O Lord, and in your great
mercy defend us from all perils and dangers of this
night; for the love of your only Son, our Savior Jesus
Christ. *Amen.*

Be present, O merciful God, and protect us through the
hours of this night, so that we who are wearied by the
changes and chances of this life may rest in your eternal
changelessness; through Jesus Christ our Lord. *Amen.*

Look down, O Lord, from your heavenly throne, and
illumine this night with your celestial brightness; that
by night as by day your people may glorify your holy
Name; through Jesus Christ our Lord. *Amen.*

Visit this place, O Lord, and drive far from it all snares of the enemy; let your holy angels dwell with us to preserve us in peace; and let your blessing be upon us always; through Jesus Christ our Lord. *Amen.*

## A Collect for Saturdays

We give you thanks, O God, for revealing your Son Jesus Christ to us by the light of his resurrection: Grant that as we sing your glory at the close of this day, our joy may abound in the morning as we celebrate the Paschal mystery; through Jesus Christ our Lord. *Amen.*

*One of the following prayers may be added:*

Keep watch, dear Lord, with those who work, or watch, or weep this night, and give your angels charge over those who sleep. Tend the sick, Lord Christ; give rest to the weary, bless the dying, soothe the suffering, pity the afflicted, shield the joyous; and all for your love's sake. *Amen.*

*Or this:*

O God, your unfailing providence sustains the world we live in and the life we live: Watch over those, both night and day, who work while others sleep, and grant that we may never forget that our common life depends upon each other's toil; through Jesus Christ our Lord. *Amen.*

*Silence may be kept, and free intercessions and thanksgivings may be offered.*

*The service concludes with the Song of Simeon:*

SUNG OR SAID BY ALL

Guide us waking, O Lord, and guard us sleeping; that awake we may watch with Christ, and asleep we may rest in peace.

*In Easter season, add* Alleluia, alleluia, alleluia.

Lord, you now have set your servant free*
    to go in peace as you have promised;

For these eyes of mine have seen the Savior,*
    whom you have prepared for all the world to see:

A Light to enlighten the nations,*
    and the glory of your people Israel.

Glory to the Father, and to the Son, and to the Holy
    Spirit:*
    as it was in the beginning, is now, and will be for ever.
    Amen

*All repeat the Antiphon.*

Guide us waking, O Lord, and guard us sleeping; that
awake we may watch with Christ, and asleep we may
rest in peace.

*In Easter season, add* Alleluia, alleluia, alleluia.

OFFICIANT
Let us bless the Lord.

PEOPLE
Thanks be to God.

THE OFFICIANT CONCLUDES
The almighty and merciful Lord, Father, Son, and Holy
Spirit, bless us and keep us. *Amen.*